STRONGER

T0345754

STRONGER

TIMOTHY KELLY

Oberlin College Press

www.oberlin.edu/~ocpress

Publication of this book was supported in part by a grant from the Ohio Arts Council.

Ohio Arts Council
A STATE AGENCY
THAT SUPPORTS PUBLIC
PROGRAMS IN THE ARTS

Library of Congress Cataloging-in-Publication Data

Kelly, Timothy
    Stronger / Timothy Kelly.
    (The FIELD Poetry Series v. 9)
    I. Title.   II. Series.

LC: 00-100940
ISBN: 0-932440-87-8 (pbk.)

The human body is the magazine of inventions, the patent office, where are the models from which every hint is taken. All the tools and engines in earth are only extensions of its limbs and senses.
—Ralph Waldo Emerson

This book is dedicated to my parents and teachers.

TABLE OF CONTENTS

I.

II.

III.

I.

STRONGER

I've got a tractor grip on his pelvis
and block his knees with mine, so that
when I arch backwards, teeter-totter-like, he's
levered up smoothly, in a pinned, reciprocal rise,
and his legs made, for one brief moment, to again
bear weight, the attendant shakes speaking briefly,
eloquently, of the distance we have yet to travel
before those legs will be strong enough to bring him,
back extending, without collapse or bracing, on
the glimmer of an impulse, up, ever again, to vertical.

Yesterday, at Staircase, Lisa and I had reached
the far point of our excursion, when the ceiling
parted unexpectedly, and the old growth, sun-shot,
lit up in swaths and diagonals, and the canopy flared
into song. We sunned a half hour on some flat
riverside boulders, grazed through the apples
and cheese, then stripped and waded, waist-deep
into the Skokomish, our feet braced hard against
the river rock and the casual, steely, god-like
power of the current. That morning, we had locked

the doors against our own kids and made rare,
fully awakened love, working at it, digging deep,
our attack and timing effortlessly, speechlessly,
in synch. Now, easing this brain-injured patient
back to his chair, I remember how the Skokomish,
in 20 seconds, had numbed us, sapped the spring

from our legs, scissoring around our bellies,
our straining thighs, our rawness. We could not

move forward even an inch against it, and eventually
dragged ourselves back out and sprawled exhausted,
exhilarated, a fingerwidth away from the twisting surge,
and slept.

TWO BONES

1. Clavicle

Pronghorn, pumphandle,
cat's paw, strut.
The heart's accessible
through the pulse
in the hollow, the lip-rest,
bite block. It turns out
on its long axis when you
raise your hand to speak,
lifts like a brow
with shrugging, hardens off
a long, pliered S,
drawn back, yielding,
apple branch espaliered
with white cloth cuffs,
to the fence.

2. Femur

Plumbed from recumbent,
the temple sways on stilts,
then walks; a pitch
and scissor at the knee,
a pistoning at the hip, a
reciprocation. Shaft
in hand, one notes

the tableleg taper,
the length of the line,
convexity, bow.
The foot's burnished,
belled, cloven; the neck
bent to a 7, knobbed.
Together, flexed to level,
they form a lap; apart,
an open question
every dog in me eyes.

REACH

Your scapula, lost continent, drifts
forward on your back, reefs
against your ribs, and when your tasked arm
wings away from your side, is fixed,
framed, *swallowed* in the raised bed
of muscle that is the shoulder girdle,
whole-cloth, contracting. With that,
the humeral head can pivot, elbow unclasp,
wrist cock, and fingers, arriving receptive
at the object in question,

grasp. The first time I saw you, you
were in a fogwhite orchard, soaked
to the skin, picking pears. And for a while,
of the million things I knew I wanted,
I wanted you, stretched out, muscular,
most. Now our kids, counting off
calendar days, ask me what I want
for Christmas, and I can't think
of a thing. It's not as if I've given up
wanting, though I'd want that, if it
were possible, certainly. It's that

I want now, at my deepest reach,
a next breath, an epiphany periodically,
your shoulder blade, shuttle-stone,
shearing by me under freckled skin.
I want to leave them something useful,

signal stars they can use to navigate,
the goods and gods grouped stars make.
I want to give back the yellow budgie
my grandmother set shaking on my finger,
its jerky, hallucinated swivel, its strangely
transported song.

RISE VS. RUN

Fallen roofer rise, I say, like some wigged Christ
to Lazarus, and, as the pieces of his pelvis knit back together,
remarkably, he does. And shows up at the clinic at five,
months later, packing a yard-long sturgeon fresh from
the Satsop, a thing I remember he said he'd do. The fish
was sheer science fiction: prehistoric, plated, battleship
gray; we butchered it on a piece of plywood in the alley
out back, tossing the majority, cartilaginous and streaky,
into the Foodliner dumpster next door. What was left,
he promised, was so delicious, that the ugly would be stricken
from my memory altogether.
                                        The man will never stand truly
upright again. He gave me two short months from the time
he could drag to standing, and we did our best. He had a family,
a business, and no desire to fine-tune locomotion with me.
Still, now, if I'm driving home and spot his truck, I'll scan
the rooflines for the silhouette and limp, curious to see that
signature, to see the fruit of my labors on high, exalted,
cleated to a steep pitch, working side to side, stapling tabs,
gaining slowly, like a climber, on the crest.
                                        I don't honk
if he's up there, for fear of startling him, for fear of triggering
another slip and shattering, long-storied fall. But I stopped once
when he was ground-level, calling him out, letting him cuss
my worthlessness, admiring his stupefying, tattoo-dimming tan.
I watched him stump down to his truck for his thermos and
smokes; he was helical, tapped like a screw; he has no rotation
in his hips, no toe-off, and curves out hard in front like a rooster

in a bluff charge. His back will be arthritic by the time he's 40; he shouldn't be able to walk, much less roof. Yet he laughs. I laugh. Black squirrels fly, in furious arcs, through the deep green yard around us. The whole thing is a complete mystery to me.

FROM NOTHING

From pitch changes carried the mile
over rooftops from the freeway, from
the hiss of the willow sketching arabesques
in wind, from the cadence of the ballgame
on the neighbor's TV, from the epileptic
down in the drugstore when I was 10,
eyes wide, jerking, as if sneezing
or trying to speak, from lawnmowers Saturdays,
from starlings plied into the eaves, from
the hard thump of bass throbbing pickups
at stopsigns, from the throttled-up lilac two
blocks away, from the stoop, at dusk, dimly,
from the sound of the furnace starting and stopping,
from the roar of the skillet when garlic's
tossed in, from my children, their breathing,
from the air, sleep, from nothing

7-INCH REVEAL

We entered, that dream, to whipsawn trombones, and wove
through a riveted grandstand while pompadoured jugglers
whipped machetes, in short, glittering arcs, back and forth
at each other below us. The parachute tent, beaten
by drafts, shook and popped, sucking in, billowing out
flabbily, like a fibrillating heart. The audience sat
transfixed, like B-grade Hollywood extras, frozen solid,
mid-gesture, by powerful alien beams. The jugglers
might have strolled between them casually, like judges
of swine at a fair, tapping their legs lightly,
with sticks, to reposition them. All this I say to you
by way

       of misdirection, as a smart infielder will freeze
a runner, looking left, squaring, starting and *selling* left,
before throwing, last possible second, right, or as our night's
conversation might begin with a brief review of the day:
a diabetic foot, a relocated elbow, a cat-like Laotian
who beats his back with hard rubber balls tied whiplike,
by strings, to a stick. He brings the device in for me to evaluate,
try. No, I say, my wife is the only one in our family
who is capable of being so direct. She has no trouble
saying I love you like they do in the movies, her eyes boring
directly into mine, the complete destruction of the earth
mere seconds away. I find myself telling him, inexplicably,
charts piling up on my desk,

                       about the night last fall
we found the hornets' nest hanging in the spiked, bony
branches of the hawthorne, and how I, despite having

every reason to believe it empty, could barely bring myself
to touch it, reaching in with a rake handle, nudging it lightly,
leaping back tachypnic every time it started to
bob. You seized the rake from me then, stepped in
and whacked the thing like a piñata, sent it flying deep
into the middle of the yard, then squatted down
next to the fractured, papery shell and held it out to me
dispassionately. It was like a bizarre, oversized Christmas
ornament, or some stray, unruly planet driven, by the laws
of physics and the force of your love, unerringly back into line.

TWO ON A SHAMAN'S RATTLE, TLINGIT, UBC MUSEUM OF MAN

1. On top, a carved green frog faces a squat, grimacing, bent-
   over-backwards man, the two of them fixed as if in mid-
   convulsion. And from one's open mouth to the other, a thin arc,
   a tapering bridge, a seamless architectural joinery of tongues.

   Two nights back, in Sooke, a chorussing of frogs had flooded
   our campsite at dusk, a din grown so loud by bedtime that it actually
   unhinged the kids. So we took our flashlights down to the water
   and unearthed a few, jewel-crusted, glistening green, who stared

   obliquely, refusing to sing in our lights. We retired then, exhausted
   but satisfied, though the singing went on, surging with each brief
   shouldering-through of the moon, moving in odd slips and gearings,
   rising and falling like Lenten litanies, like long evening prayer

   in a foreign language washing over the tourist hotel. Everyone
   slept but me, who lie there irredeemably wired, the song rising
   in waves through the ground, buzzing inside my skull, my chest,
   my heart sagging, thrilling, my tongue, as if in a current, twitching.

   I must've drifted off before moonset though, because I woke later
   into pure ink-black, startled, I slowly realized, by the suddenly
   lengthening silence. I remember waking that way in 1973, in Lisa's
   father's Electra, in a Pentacostal church parking lot in Roanoke,

   after a night of broke and desperate wandering. We'd found
   the place providentially, in the middle of the night unlocked, and

made clutching, standing-up love just inside the back doors, in
shapeshifty, echoing dark. We figured it had been hours, at most,

since the Spirit had come, lightning-like, through that very spot,
since His vessels, electrified, had sung out syllable after delirious
syllable, the congregation closing tightly around them, hands
heavenward, in praise. We, however, had one more featureless hour

until my bus, and no sense that the two of us belonged anywhere
in the mathematical universe. I remember birdsong, like faint, hallucinated
conversation, opening up from the near trees, and bolting up wildeyed,
scrambling to find the keys to fire the ignition to lower the windows

to face what I was sure would be police, or pistol-stiffened pastor,
or a carful of her bullnecked brothers, patience exhausted, homing in
on their prodigal and her latest acid-jacked pencil sketch of a man.

2. The streaming sun, finally cresting the ridge, works down through
   the trees like a benediction. And the silverbacked cedars behind us,
   suddenly spotlit, spring rows of thin, wagging tongues, night's breath
   exhausted, in slow jets and ripples, back into air. They rise and

   disappear. Last night I dreamt of a foraging animal shifting soundlessly
   through these trees, and it struck me finally that it was not you, that
   it would never *be* you again. I softened my shoulders and turned to it,
   yielding, willing. I wanted though, more than anything, to get up

and *go out to* it, to track it along the littered forest floor, to come up
on it quietly and circle it, stepping up to it and stepping back
in what slowly would become a dance, and singing low, calming
syllables across its bent neck, across the rhythm of my shaking

hand, where the shaman's rattle chattered and hushed, the light alive
in the intricate relief, the bottled stars inside swirling and crashing,
bright shot raining back and rebroadcast, by birdlike flicks
of the wrist, into the dark drumming dome of the sky.

DON'T MEAN A THING IF

When she raises her arm to block the blow, grit
in the gearbox, a withering stab. The move curves
from her center, like some thin steely whisker,
but her pain's at the pivot, the ball-peened *point*
of her shoulder, and patent neglect, to date,
hasn't worked. Age, breasts, long life conspires
to pull those shoulders further forward each year,
and her upper back, once rake-handle straight, is,
she's noticed, starting to dome. Her arm, loaded,
levered to the horizon, fails; she says Tell me
the things this could be. In the book of the body,

we find the skeleton, and the skeleton progressively
overlain, etched densely, all angles, with muscle:
pulleys, cables, winches, sheets; *rhomboids, levator,*
middle traps. The bone-loom, tensioned by section,
rises, locomotes, the basic mechanics providing
us, always, a template, strategy, start. Yes, she nods,
following, but what about the *chi* of the thing,
pegged meridians lit, the flow of energy, blocked?

My first Saturday in Seattle, I watched a dozen people
move together an hour in sun, gracefully repeating
pieces of a long *Tai Chi* form in a park on a hill,
gi's flowing, crows slotting the firs, gawkers
and dog-walkers idling courteously on the fringe.
And to to my back, the looming mountain, brilliant,

finely faceted, a single lenticulate cloud suspended
above it, a vested and haloed god sitting balanced,
breath moving, not contemplating speech.

TRACTION

1. She has a pain in her arm like biting
   on foil, and for a week has had to sleep
   sitting up, braced, bolstered, cooped in
   her chair, breathing in short sips, all but
   the most gathered movements electrifying.
   But traction to her neck, our opening
   strategy, utterly, *deus ex machina,* relieves it.
   So we dim the lights and leave her there,
   lying back, tied in, smiling skeptically,
   tears welling, brimming, slowly soaking
   the sides of the cradling head-halter dark.

   But in 30 minutes, when I slacken the pull
   and sit her back up, the pain, as I'd feared,
   returns, branching down, jagged, hot, like
   ginseng, or lightning strikes burned, in
   fractured multiples, onto film. And she begins
   to rock in place like a wild thing, shaking
   off touch, moaning notes, slapping her
   left arm with her right, as if there were
   things the guttering left needed to hear,
   and the right was, at long last, willing
   to say.

2. The most I hope to accomplish
   is to gap the joint enough
   to let the thinnest picket of light
   in, to slip the stick out
   of the dog's locked jaw,

to pry the edge of the rock
a short, wedgeable half-inch
up. Underneath, carnival

movement: beetled spins
and midway scurrying. And
the patient will stare off,
transfixed, as if at some
epiphany, as if at the missing
piece of an echoing puzzle
he'd long ago given up trying
to solve.

3. 22 vertebrae stacked
   like blocks on a shelf,
   curving out, in, and
   out again, like a standing
   wave, or a leaf spring,
   loaded. And above all,
   the head, heavy as
   a bowling ball, borne up
   like a gem-crusted relic at
   the head of a high-holy-days
   parade. In my notes

   I say she's improved,
   able to look right,
   to raise her right arm,

to sleep in a bed again.
And to dream, she says.
Wildly, she says, a lead

I must technically let drift
by. Already, in another
room, a new patient waits,
foot crushed to chalk-stubs
weeks ago by her own
ditzy teenager in her own
narrow driveway by her
own swerving car, and
sawn, just yesterday, out
of its battered club of a cast.
The foot is stiff, prickly,
wooden; she no longer has
an acceptable interface,

a satisfactory link
to the world. The foot
does not propel her
gracefully forward.
She is reminded of
dreams where you run,
arms, legs moving,
clattering, whirling, and
within it, like the throat
of a lily slowly opening,
the realization that you've
gone nowhere.

EARTHQUAKE, WITH RECONSTRUCTED LEG

10th floor, Harborview M.C., Seattle

The tinctured thing lay across my lap, the light violet
they paint them at surgery, the weeping, boglike length
of it a welter of staples and stitches. I'd been tapping
the thigh to get trace contractions, tapping in time
with hard-cadenced commands: Melissa, straighten
your leg. Melissa. Straighten. No use. She's slipped
down into a head-lolled, post-op, Percocet dream.

Beyond the curtain, the paras roll, mouths running,
into the gym, boomboxes bungied to the backs
of their chairs. Near the weight stacks, Prince's *Jam*
of the Year opens tripping and uncontested, and I know
without looking they'll dance, the room tumbling
section by section, chairs sawn through low spins
and crescents, a coiled arm suspended overhead,
dreamlike, the gunshot, the motorcycle-crashes,
dark-lashed local gods, freshly cut in half, chugging,
reciprocating, bearing down, purse-lipped, in synch.

I remember the look of the light at 3, windows green,
rain-raked, and a wind off the Sound I could feel
myself stuggling home against, soon. When
the shake and swaying stopped, one ceiling tile
hung. I expected shouts. Instead, someone casually
clicked off the music. I felt as if I were perched
on a precipice, as if all I needed to do was tip forward
to pitch, arms out, over the world, where everything

I love was laid out below me, vivid and clarified,
the way the enormous dimensions of a room are
clarified as trembling anger's, in stinging lengths, let go.

II.

THE ENCHANTMENTS, SEPTEMBER

A day's climb brings us up to the shot granite basin, nickel
lakes scattered, the stunty larches in gold climax, ringing.
A windfall, still rooted, a trembling tightrope-walk out

over *black,* where sunlight, split to shafts, slants, shifts,
the day's heat, my hand held in. Should I pitch camp now,
before the closing storm breaches the near ridge carbureted

and steep, or shed clothes and boots and launch out fully
into prayer? Trout, backs lit, deep, glint green. And
thunder, still distant, pacing gods clearing their throats

to swallow, or sing.

AT PACIFIC RIM

Each small stream we picked our way across
that week was choked red and vivid with salmon,
the spent floating torn and streaky, the living
flapping over the backs of the dead. Then,

especially then, we felt we understood the obliterating
call to spawn; what finally seemed the miracle,
though, was the navigation: how each, by some
perfect admixture of taste, topography, and stars

found his way back, memory unreeling, out of gray-scale
ocean, to the exact landfall, the precise drainage, the creek
fork, gravel bank, spawning bed, zeroing, burrowing,
home. We thought then of our favorite dying patients

back in Seattle, the lucky few looming death turns clear,
energized, determined, tender; *we* would live that way,
we decided then, always; forever. It was a prayer, our first,
one we repeat Sunday, years later, at Kennedy Creek

where we take our boys to see the dwindling silvers
run. The two of them, sprung, rocket off like dogs,
diving into brush, mapping terrain, nosing methodically
upstream. We find a vantage, a glassy pool, and wait

for a black hump to jet across the current, to razor up,
in cursive, a message about the other life, the one that
gestures below the surface of this one; the one that
abrupts into dreams; the one coincidence touches

a toe to, and wisdom wells up from, pulsed, eccentric;
the one whose design we pray properly to know, and
whose answers stream by daily: hieroglyphic, glinting,
and utterly, in the end, beyond us. Our single bedrock

commandment is to make a home for these boys; but
we both believe that one day, in the blur of random motion,
one of us will lock on a sign or cipher and veer, pure impulse,
pure trajectory, galvanized, clarified, swallowing, *sure.*

TWO LOVE POEMS

1. Seven herons, slate, shin-deep,
   stockstill, staring into what's swirled
   by them on the ebb. This is how

   I knew I would never leave you:
   the stab, blink, the stilletoed head tipped
   backwards, the quick, coiled neck stretched
   skyward, to swallow.

2. I dreamt the kids gone, and you,
   careful, reaching through apple branches
   with a long-handled torch,
   burning caterpillar tents. My anger,
   deep mystery, was gone, and I flew
   forward twenty yards with every step.

   I had a rainbow on a stringer,
   still kicking, to show you, grabbed him,
   lost him, grabbed him, lost, etc. You,
   laughing, the pole-end, flaming.
   I wanted every remaining day to be
   with you, slow as surfacing, slow
   as the last inch of honey, slower.

TURNING HEADS

She's in a gown and supine, and her neck
is in my hands, the beatings, car-wrecks,
the skittish Arab fell hard on her when she was 10,
the stiff list of insults recited, acknowledged, set
behind us again in a neat, algebraic line. Now, I say,
Let me have this head. The neck's *motion;* the joints'
subtle locking, unlocking, distractions and glides:
these things speak. But they can't say a thing unless
you let go. So here. Let's try. Deep breath. Ah.

Let go. Last summer, shot, sleepwalking through
the Uffizi on our last day in Florence, I found myself
in front of Cellini's *Perseus and Medusa* transfixed,
the arcade sunlit, the beauty of the thing more penetrating
with each unsteadied step. He was more perfect
than David, I thought, holding her slacklidded head
aloft, while at his feet, her flawless trunk slumped,
the stump of her neck a frank, oddly accurate section
of sinew, gristle and bone. It reminded me of your neck

the night before as you read in the garden, hair upswept,
pinned for dinner, the last of the sun highlighting
the strong, graceful line of the curve. I had the urge
to go to it, to visit briefly, in braille, the variety of
small knots I've helped put there, and have, despite
unstinting disavowals, come to know by heart.
But you turned toward me then, long neck muscles

reconfigured, face and senses leveled optimally
to process whatever thing, separating from the periphery,
as yet unappraised, approached.

VOLUPTUARY

A siren, a taut, singing line jerks me
up, nose-first, in a tightening spiral,
the dreamt conversations, the honeyed,
half-familiar rooms shrinking backwards,
yawning off, as the two of them
scramble over our legs and backs and
work down, all grunts and giggles
between us.
                 I remember waking
in Cincinnati, years ago, in a cold
so profound that the river froze solid
bank to bank, and the barges, disbelieving,
within it; and you could walk out,
as we did, in twos and threes, and stand
half in Ohio, half in Kentucky, and
watch the traffic struggle by above you,
clanking, the highbeams rippling
jewel-like through the bridgework
overhead.
              What *is* there now
except bellies and butts, and drooling
and elbows and hard heels wedged in
for warming? What is there except
them, green-boned, taut-lipped, racing
teary for a stand of trees, branches
drooping low to catch them up, trees
they tag and sprint away from, into

thronged and hissing streets, which
they cross, like quick thrusts of a knife,
without looking?

TWO GUY THINGS

1. Bringing it

All day they've been *bringing heat,* as the *cognescenti* say,
sorting and winging river rocks, palm sized, rocket-like,
skimming them off the face of the river, or rifling them
full across at the dragging, river-bobbed pennants of moss.
They've allowed me my book all morning, trout rod bobbing
indifferently across my knees. I eye them at intervals, slyly,
taken, past all else, by the mechanics of it: the drape and dip
of the shoulder, the left leg thrown up, the swivel, the thrust,
the long step forward, the arm whiplike, flashing, the wrist
snapping sharply off, for spin, for color, for punctuation.
The pattern of that raveling, and the reciprocal flying apart,
drifts through my mind like an afterimage, like the hem
of a delicious dream you want, in the midst of waking, to tug
back, to reconstruct, turning it over and over, like a key
in a lock, and praying for that sweet, breathtaking click
of readmission. This is what it is

to have them, flattening the washed clothes into piles
next to where they sleep, the long bodies, like green sticks
laid out at odd angles, jutting and jittery even at rest. There's
an encyclopedia of motions one dreams of teaching: caress
and cradle; the subtle softenings, tilts and half-turns signalling
receptiveness, yielding, yes. But there's also the reaching back
and letting fly, with increasing accuracy, over longer and longer
distances, the wide variety of projectiles, agents of change,
messages to the world, simple and direct. By three, the two

of them are naked, backlit, kneedeep in the river, lobbing
small boulders in my direction, working on placement, closing in
on the near-perfect water's edge detonation which will finally
douse and move me, the soaked book laid aside, their scramble
away a fireworks, a whirligig of music and glitter and screams.

2. Heaven

We park for an hour on the hill above the port
and watch the grapple-loaders crawl, bee-like, iridescent,
blanketing the landing, staging logs high in cotton candy
clouds of bark-dust, their diesel pitches sliding together

in odd, signatureless, twelve-tone chords, *adagio,
diminuendo.* We are here because grandpa is dying and
mom has flown off to him, here to eat pizza; here because
this is our secret place, where mythic two-story machines

shudder earth, where we can be dumb-struck, transported,
watching stoic operators move mountains of wood all night
with tiny, indecipherable flicks of their wrists. I bring up
dying as a question here, the what it is, the why it has to be,

but they are unshakably cool, pat: The rain forest they chime,
the natural succession of species; black beetles boring into
weakened cedars, and sprouts pushing up, in tough, wiry
waves through the duff. These are my words, incredible,

which they now turn blithely back on me. They take
an interest, in the end, only in the idea of *cemeteries,* of
throttled-up backhoes biting cleanly through sod, turning out
row after row of neat, narrow graves for the steady stream

of new dead people, who are carried out in shiny coffins
and planted in front of their families, like huge, hard-shelled
alien seeds. OK Dad they say finally, meaning enough
talk. And they press forward into the smeared windows

again, signalling they will brook no more questions,
drawn off, in the pearled sodium lights, by the movement,
the music, the huge, businesslike, downshifting monsters
lumbering and roaring, just beneath us, unawares.

RELIGIOUS EXPERIENCE, GARDEN VARIETY

1. Tomatoes

They shine in their jars like planets
and moons telescoped into small, dim
rooms. The scrubbed kitchen, bloody
theater, ticks now, cooling; their lids,
by evening, snap down. All summer
I tied their flail arms to the stake, hearts
on their sleeves, too much to bear. Now,
separated, cored, scalded and skinned,
they float above corruption. Outside,
the pillaged garden wilts, and a hard gilt-
edge threads itself through the bordering
woods and field, and sets the west
windows, for a moment during dinner,
on fire.

2. Corn

Rustle and clack. The tasseled sea,
sanctified and wind-worked, bends
like a choir in sway. Willowy girls
wander into the river to bathe.
Pharaoh's daughter cocks her head,
peers into the bullrushes. Moses bobs
there, tightly swaddled, in his ark
of rushes and pitch.

3. Potatoes

Archeology. Phrenology.
Something appreciated by hand, stealthily,
under the dark blue skirt of earth. Braille,
exploded. Lisa, white-breasted, blinding,
circling the garden; the long-tined fork heeled
into the hill. All our worldly wants and needs.
Grave robbers, mud-caked, huddled in a drill.
A shower of small planets, sanded smooth
in the bend of their plunge, unearthed
by accident, ages after impact, near Omaha.

LIKE RAIN DOES

Pools, face up,
restored and serene, as if come
through a long siege
of battery or bombardment unscathed.

Widens, if lashed and supine
earth is saturated, or
hardened, for the time,
against drink.

Vanishes, like a buck
from a dense blind by sunrise,
drawn deeper, leaving nothing—
the faintest depression—

WELL

What *transpires* above us in the piped-up pale of leaves
draws water, tense as harp strings, two stories up
through root, trunk, and branch, and divides it exactingly,
at the height of the climb, one fine thread per leaf. How
much more perfected, then, is the body of this 7-year-old
squatting blue-lipped next to the pumphouse, hosing down
the cider press. A minute ago, grinding apples, he told me
about the Mormon boys on mountain bikes he's been seeing,
canvassing the city for a solid year in suits, ringing doorbells and
planting their seed (he said) in converts. I think of the apprehension

of the world, the barrage of bewildering information transformed,
broken to bits, coded by senses, converging on the center,
rising heavenward, trimmed and filtered, in the long pliant
wand of the spine. I think of barrel fires, the up-twist of smoke;
I think of prayer. I think, when the pump trips on behind us,
of the sterling column of water, pencil-lead-like, drawn up,
in that hum, from the earth; of its steady rise and icy end,
splashing limp from the hose-stem over our flat-pink, cider-
sticky hands. I notice, in the dusk, the roses Lisa and I planted
years ago along the street-side of the pumphouse, lying now
in a fall-blotched tangle of bony stems and hips. I think of
a patient I had last spring in the ICU, a leukemic, a hard stick

of a boy, who asked me one day to help him pull the wire screen
off his window. And when I did, he pushed open the glass
and walked over a dozen of those smug, indestructible mylar
balloons, which sailed up, ribbon-tailed and sputnik-like, into

the May afternoon. We watched them a good ten minutes, as they shrank into pinpoint blue nothing, and a little longer still. Then I clipped the screen back on, put him back to bed, scribbled some fiction in his chart, tapped the button and waited for the crowded lunchtime elevator to crack open, tip me in, and transport me, in its tranced, hydraulic chain of fits and starts, up.

URGENCY

I stand her on her new pinned
hip, the day already a shambles,
and because I'm rushing, and have
neglected to ask her, she immediately,
because it is the law, has to pee. So
I roll over the commode, ease her
back down, wrap a loose sheet
around her middle and cinch her
tight to the chair, fixed upright,
knotted in, and step back out into
traffic and the litany of pages,
and sag in the jamb, blocked,
drumming, waiting for her call.
                                    But
suspended there, minutes ticking,
my breathing deepens, and my mind
begins its slow overland bounding
toward you, like the doe we caught,
years ago, in our headlights
on Orcas, coiling and lifting into
the elegant, dreamlike arc of her
leap, its phosphorous tracing,
the clutterdown fence falling,
falling slowly away, her skying
eye a black, glancing
jewel.
        She stayed
in the sky then, like a Chagall
as I recall, the two of us rough,

green and smiling, a wash of stars
and bony, blue-coated fiddler
stirred in. I would go a long way
to feel like that again, tingling,
struck like a bell, transported,
briefly, somewhere beyond
speech, beyond caring
about speech. It's a need
that brims still, that builds,
pressing, for months sometimes,
because we have dressed up and
gone to work, phones bristling
in our ears, and forgotten why
exactly it is we live.

HISTORY

There's a fly in the room.
There's the thought of you not pursuing me
but working different angles, side to side,
high up. I'm writing about the pear trees:
the espalier, limbs extended, wrists bound
loosely to the fence, while a yard away,
its twin gestures extravagantly, gathering
birds to its chest. An hour later I've climbed
shoeless, jaws clenched, onto the table with
a rolled-up newspaper in my hand.

TWO ARGUMENTS

1. I exit the freeway because of your cut,
    and a hard bile wicks the tightened rope
    of my throat, spitting bitter, blind, all out
    of proportion, as if slowing the car made
    screaming safe. Then, just as suddenly,
    I'm spent, shaky, spiralling disconnectedly
    down. It occurs to me, distantly, that
    the radio's still on, the music shot through,
    whitewashed with static. I reach, try to
    adjust it, make it worse. You reach over
    and snap it off. We are stuck then,

    for a long while, on Marginal, collateralized,
    shunted, paralleling the flow. We crawl
    block by block, light to light, in a clear,
    dreamy silence, as if suspended in glycerin,
    and dragging, at the end of a thin dancing chain,
    the very thing we set out so determinedly
    from the house to escape.

2. Odd that the argument
    carries in it the same heat
    as lovemaking, though hotter, and
    a little less long. And, too, that
    finishing leaves us flushed, stunned,
    unsure how, again, to resume. We

once crawled into a 30-foot
cedar snag in Coos Bay, Oregon,
the core burned out ages ago
by lightning, the cylinder walls
intricately etched and charcoaled. We
stood up in it carefully, not touching
anything, as if in church. And felt
ourselves drawn immediately
to the bright blue disc above us,
that blown and variegated iris, crossed
periodically by wisps of cloud-hem
or edge, which we used to construct,
in equally predictable ways, our own
competing versions of the sky.

RECESSIONAL

Coons came culling in the corn last night,
flattening the last few stalks still left standing
with ears. And I, my hand suspended a long
second above the chrome car-door handle,
feel the season, deep inside me, like a
dry stick,
        snap. Could it be time already
to strip the tangled beds, to yank out blackened
vines; to feed cut cornstalks, joint by joint,
to Ralph's crush of cattle through the fence?
Is it time to heave the misshapen, sunlike
pumpkins up, and stump them one by one,
clutching them to my belly, to the porch?

III.

AT 40

I've left the trees far
below me and breathing
labors like a dull saw, hot
and binding. When I rest,

my handbook tells me
what, at this elevation, grows:
sedums, lichen, lowlying,
stunty junipers and heather.

The closer we dare
approach the sun, the more
thoroughly planed and scoured
the rock; and yet what does

persist here blooms spectacularly,
defiantly, thrusting bright
flags up into insensible
clarity and violence.

LIGHT, EASTER

The bones proceed
from the pelvis
like planets from
the sun, the chimney
stack spine, lines
of the limbs, the skull
a white tablet
the sifting weather
of the face plays over.
We are a picnic moved

steadily up-yard
by lengthening
shade, still chill,
the sentinel daffs
choiring collared,
the sun-throttled
daphne, bee-worked,
yielding. I am moved

repeatedly to the
dowels and pegs
of your hands'
dancing, the knuckles'
swell, tendons'
tension, the starry
freckles, in lapped
constellations,
compounding. For

six months, darkness,
then this: sirens and
siphoning, liquid
seeking, the glinting
cruet Magdelene
shepherded to the tomb,
to the washed and
bluing body, the sheen
thumbed tenderly
onto curled palms,
stilled lids, lips.

ACOLYTES: SERVING 6:30 MASS

We've lit the nave from the breakers, and all the tall
altar candles, and slouch panda-like, black and white,
in our cassocks and surplices, waiting for our man,
Fr. Hanzo, the berator, the prick, the invariably-hung-over

to show. And when he does shuffle in, sour-smelling,
hack-shaven, we circle and vest him, cincture and alb,
while he stands like Christ crucified, eyes rolled back,
arms out, half-conscious, rocking. We ring the bells,

we march, we get through it. And filing back in, we
flatten ourselves against the sacristy wall, and he sweeps by
and does not bless us, staggering instead for his coffee
and Luckies, and yesterday's racing results. Fuck him

we say out loud in the hall to the next crew, nodding.
Fuck *him* we say genuinely, heatedly, again and again,
until laughter finally shoulders in, blunts us, and we rehang
our vestments mimicking him, perfecting, by turns, the lisp

and scowls of the pillar of Fairview, the confessor
of widows, the place-loser, the dimwit, the one who
convinces us finally, viscerally, that the road to sainthood
is far too tortured, lined as it is with figures we cannot help

but despise. We cross Lorain, still a river of headlights,
to AmyJoy Donuts, every blurted, every hard, mangled phrase
of Mass Latin sending us now into stratospheric, helpless,
asphyxiating spasms of laughter. We stake out a table

among the black-fingered machinists from Ford, who
come here every morning on their way home from graveyard
to read *Plain Dealers* and translate things the hard-blonde
waitresses say into Polish. We figure maybe they are

the saints, waiting for their curlered wives to clear out
the house, the night's shower of metal shavings still
embedded in their arms and heads, glittering like tinseled trees
when they raise up their cups, consecration-like, to signal

the slouching clutch of waitresses, sharing a quick smoke
at the end of the scarred, hatcheted counter, One more.

ON THE SLIDE

for Emmett

I owned this town once, I call down
to your mother, who smiles in acknowledgment,
I think. And from my commanding height, the leggy
water tower, chalkwhite capitol, the fog-switched town
fall steadily away, hill by thumbprinted hill, to the south.
What, I wonder, did I spend all those years out there *doing*
before you? I think of the photo I keep above my desk
at work, one I glance at often between patients: it's
summer; you bursting out of sunflowers, saucer-eyed,
laughing; me behind you, lunging in pursuit. Something
drawn in my look, something puny about the drape
or wing of my shoulder; some frank, offhanded voice, deep
in my head, the first time I saw it, said *That guy*

is old. I remember we carried pillows out, the night
of that chase, to Ralph's field for sunset. The grass
was fresh-cut, sweet, the haying just in, and we lay there
together a long time, you interviewing your endlessly
quotable self, and watched the swallows shear by dizzily
overhead, their swoops and stalls breathtaking, their stunt-
dives reminding me, in the mercurochromed dusk, of falls
which kill old people, the falls which killed Ike and Ellen
Curry, our neighbors, in storybook fashion that spring:
first him, and then, improbably, a short month later,
her. I had to stand her, at work, on her second day
in the hospital, her new pinned hip shaky, her fingers
around my arms like vicegrips, her lungs half-filled
with fluid, her beautiful, sculpted face upturned to me

in bewilderment. Gravity brought down our photogenic ·
sunflowers too, not long after that day, their lion-heads
nodding, exhausted, earthward. And we hacked them off,
you and I, machete-man and his apprentice machete-boy,
and nailed them, seedy-side-up, to Ralph's fenceposts
for the long succession of southering birds to lock on
and flock to, dropping one by one, feet-first, all fall,
out of the slanted, glinting, quarter-colored sky.

MANIPULATING THE INNOMINATES

I stand her aching back against the wall,
the bony landmarks highlighted beforehand
in pen, and compare her to a simple plumb
line. The object is to illuminate the symmetry
of her pelvis, that most beautiful conjunction
of bones, that perfect funnel, that radiant angel
kneeling, wings extended, in the exact sentry-center
of the stoneyard. To fully appreciate it, I describe
a brisk ellipse around her, noting cant,
camber, list and line. Then, regardless
of irregularity, I kneel down in front of her,
grasp the flared innominates, and twist clockwise,
counterclockwise, looking back to her face for
a shrug or scowl. We move then, accordingly,
to supine or prone, to hip extension, to bridging,
to the *sort* of telling contortions, to ruling in, to
talking out, to tacking down the planks of a corrective
plan. But the first step is always the sober standing
still, a squatting stranger staring squarely into
the sanctuary, the tabernacle door propped
open, the dog-penned world nosing brightly in
for a look. They may not, for the moment, close
the gown. They bear my scrutiny, squirming,
for a price: they want, in the end, their wages,
my verdict, the solid, conjuring word; that thing's
been stabbing them—they want to know *its name.*

A SHORT AFTER-DINNER
ARGUMENT AMONG DOCTORS
ABOUT THE WORST WAYS TO DIE

They trump each other's nominees
grimly, graciously, stacking dishes and
buttressing details in downgoing August
light. Into this contest, announced
by shouting, trots Keats, masked finch
clamped in his jaws, trailing a line
of riveted, mildly disturbed kids.
Black cat, yellow feathers, blue carpet;
the room stills, then stops short
for one struck moment, perfectly
balanced. Then the cat tips just
out of reach, hunkers down whiptailed,
and growls. The finch's one free wing twitches.

DIVING INTO THE SOUND

In church, after the last blessing, as the priest
cued his exit and the choir stiffened aloft,
I would twist, my mother's hand on my collar,
to watch the great doors walked open, and the day,
gold-veined, leaf-green, spin ecstatically, hems
billowing, back in. But this is the opposite:

a flinty flash like a blow to the head; starry
night, and swallowing. If I knew what drew me

down, if my tarry, crow-raftered soul
could be lofted on some unison updraft of prayer,
I would sit out gladly, with the annointed, and bask.
But when I work my way down to water, water
lit, lapping, lashed with color, I feel buoyed, bowed,
and long to lay out over it, to leave parched earth,
to go headlong through flashing light and crash

cold, stopped, suspended, into dream. The rent
in heaven heals above me, glittering. I hear nothing:
grace note; rest. Then the paired, shuddering
blows of my heart's reassertion. And then, *only*
then, the faint trills and bellringing water's always used
to smooth shivering, to soothe stunned strangers,
to sanctify the seeker held down, beneath loud praying,
in his sputtering baptismal plunge.

PHYSICAL THERAPY

My swimmer's positioned hands up, standing, a flat
wash of daylight across her back, the v-shaped field
simplified, balanced, but underwritten by a deeper
pattern, a fluid muscular *set* that changes expression
with each graceful shift of her linked trunk and arm.
For a month, it's pained her right shoulder to crawl.

In a minute, when she's supine, we'll range and scour
the shoulder, distract the humerus on its long axis, and
translate the bone's loose, halfmoon head forward&back
in its ground-down socket, shallow as a palm, shallow
as the cove you and I kayaked into last August, near
Eastsound, on a bathlike, spat-streaked, midday tide.

We beached by a saltstreaked madronna, turned and dove
back upchannel, stroking out strong, cadenced, shoulder
to shoulder, then turned onto our backs, to rest. A kingfisher
shot over us, chattering, then struck twice just beyond,
tight explosions hanging briefly inside the lapped,
shimmering stylus-line of shade. We dried draped raglike

over the ribs of that tree, rust bark peeling papery, and
a flare of yellow sedums reaching upland, brimming bees.
I put a spray of cedar in my pocket that afternoon,
thinking of my father, thinking of the soul, at the Last
Judgment, reunited with the body. It will be strange,
after so many years, to stand again, shaky, on coltish,

resurrected legs, to reach in my pocket and crush
the cedar between my palms, to lift them turpentined,
as the crying and sorting out begins, to my face, his, yours.

IS THIS LEG LOVELY?

she asks when I've undone the gauze and splinting
and laid it across my arms. And I say, flexing the knee,
Yes, it is. And since it's her first visit, I measure and chart
the range of her ankles, knees, and hips, the long, vertical
scars still bristled with stitches, the brushed violet edging,
the blue, swollen, too cool foot. Tonight, under stars, I will

scan north, over trees, for the spiral stick, the splayed W
that is Casseopeia, and it will remind me of this hard,
carpentered leg, of her accordioned car and the unmoved tree,
of the lightning bolt the rabbit in her headlights described,
or the bent old woman she dreamt on her morphine drip,
who unlooped his snared foot, cooing, then slit his throat

for stew. It will never be simple again, this leg, I tell her,
because it's the kindest truth at hand. And I add We'll get
through it, meaning the repetitions, the giving way, the tremors
and falls, and the rising unaided, at great long last, from
a chair. But past that, her grief still throttling, I'm useless,
fenced, and drift back, by habit, to Avon, to the silver silo

off Rte.10, where my cousins' dogs worked the stubble fall
Saturdays for rabbits, and lovers came nightly to watch stars
wrap up the dim tinny curve of its sides. I know I've left
something there, and begin circling, head down, looking for
my signal, some cindery glint in the grass; while behind me,
the blunt thing rises flat-seamed, heavenward, clanging.

DRIVING IN RAIN

We remember the trip
as whole cloth, unreeling
from a bolt, and forget
how the blunt drops
obliterated the world, and
how all we had, really,
were split-seconds
of clarity, the quick slash
of wipers, measure and
blur. These we stitch
together, like we do
dreams we can only
remember three or four
fragments of, holding
them curved in one hand,
morning brightening,
running the combinations,
waiting for the seam,
for the path *in* to appear,
for the road to rise up
timely, mile after mile,
even with our guessing.

A WALK TO THE FAIR

I'm crossing a rust and green field in Lacey at Easter
with an old patient, ex-cop, hip fracture, plate and pins,
slowly, because he limps, towards the stacked lights,
screams and calliope music rising brazen, Oz-like, out
of the cindery, colonized Priest Point Park parking lot.

He vaults, circumducting the planed leg, lifting it out
and spearing it down, shiver reverberating shin, leg,
spine, his trunk sidebent to compensate the stiff,
compass-leg sweep of the hip, his head and shoulders
rung up, at the end of each stroke, in rote, summary

punctuation. We part at the *Trabant*, bulb-ridged rays
splayed out, spin up, crowd parting around us,
the sifting-down dusk dense with smokes, cologne,
popcorn, and a funky, unmistakable note of skunk cabbage
wafting in glimmers from the park's own wetlands, but

blooming everywhere this week, in creekbottoms,
woodlots, leaflitter, as if some switch had been thrown,
stems spiralling a foot overnight, great, waxy leaves
unfurled, pillowed back to reveal the yellow, cob-like
flower erect, iridescent, lotuslike, blazing deep in

the latticed understory, each a fixed signal, lit kindling.
This is the month when the frank scent of sex edges
everything, when each body's secret, winterworked
shrine's revealed, moving hublike at the center of *gait,*
that reciprocating sequence, interrupted fall, insinuating

signature more peculiar, more patently memorable
than words. Years on, when you can no longer recall
names, or the strains of conversation, you'll still see,
in etched, eloquent detail, the pivotal gesture, slant of eye,
her wordless rising and determined striding away.

ANNIVERSARY

A sea lion perched on reef rocks
near Vashon Landing bellows, anticipating,
we guess, our ferry's arrival blast. And
when it comes, echoing hard off the cliffs,
we walk astern once more to take in that
ancient, whiskered, bullet-like head, swiveling.
We had been talking about the glass
we dug out of Cole's foot last Saturday,
and the odd necessity of inflicting pain,
on occasion, to relieve it. You gave me
my choice of jobs matter-of-factly:
hold him or dig with the needle. I dug.

I remember the spell, years ago now,
when we, without speaking, would strap
the boys in the car and drive, windows wide,
out into the country, letting them wail
their exhausted wails, letting the cries
wash out over the flat, harrowed fields,
while we sat mute, lost in the narrow,
hissing, lit fuse of road. It was then

I began piling up complaints against you
like kindling at the bound feet of a witch.
What saved us, I think now, were those rare,
unchoreographed moments when we managed,
for an instant, to turn our gazes simultaneously
outward to the scrawled drawing, the cat-gouged

flicker, the sarcococus coming into improbable,
intoxicating February flower. Now, the world

we once wanted to save saves us. And
as we stand at the rail, rolling slightly,
next to two teenagers wound in a tight,
overheated farewell clinch, we do not look
at one another. I put my hand lightly
on the small of your back, in thanks,
and we watch wave after wave rise up
and smash into the rocks behind us, thudding
like cannon, spray sailing up, slow-

motion, like fireworks. Then
below us, on the car deck, engines catch
and rev, and offloading begins, the tight strands
slowly separated, another disordered knot
undone; and the line of cars begins its steady
streaming up, with ceremonial honks and waves,
into the steep, wind-waxed island woods.

SETTING TILE

We mopped off the curing's
dust, rescribed our marks, and
snapped a line; the dull white slab
stung diagonally, cuechalk blue, fine.
Above us,

too high to hear, a glint of jet,
like a stray remark, pulled a taut
white thread across an otherwise
unmarked sky. A minute of morning passed by.
And as you turned

to speak to me, a bee
wove up from the dark, fluted throat
of the calla lily and paused in a lip of light,
his forelegs slashing back, combing over and over
mouth and face and eyes,

his back legs caked in saffron,
and dragging.

EXPLODED VIEW

Light laid out, in huge honeyed blocks, across campus.
Below me, the day nurses, making for their cars.
I've taken down my *Gray's Anatomy* to recheck the order
of the bones in the wrist, notched and rising in their tight
architectural arch, whose names I have never, for some reason,
been able to keep straight.
                  I'm working up the wrist
of an arthritic pianist, a snow-dotted fall on an outstretched
hand, which splinting and medicine have so far failed to solve.
Her films are clean. Her tendons, traced back through
the narrow cinch of her wrist, glide. But she cannot play Bach,
cannot execute the hard hammering, the combinations, cannot
make the pieces run headlong, as they must, the avalanche
of notes driven forward, flurried and relentless, each *arpeggio,*
each falling figure sealing over the last.
                        The cumulative effect,
at the end of the day, is of syncope, drift: Vermilion buried
in a sugarbowl, the dazzling lake groaning and stiffening; of
slow fusion, blurred edges, slipped traction, and silence stretching
until I find my page, and music starts up again: *trapezius,*
trapezoid, triquetral, the world laid out once more before me
comfortingly, crisply, part-after-stamped-out-part, music box-like.
I can *deal* with this, I think, staring into the works,
                            the gears
and bushings, levers and pulleys drawing me down, rising
around me, clutching into their slow, contrapuntal spins, their
quartz-edged, tethered pony-walks around me, the symmetry
of the turnings stunning, dance-like, nearly divine, the music
masking the movement, the movement music itself.

HOH LAKE CODA

We've attained the divide
in daylight, despite multiple stops
at pools to plunge, and made camp
in a saddle with lilies, the nested lake,
pie-tin glinty, tailing down at the edges
a steep, mineral, milk-tinged blue.

Ten years ago we woke here
to elk: bulls mewing in the ramparts,
cows bending primly, heads together,
to drink. And when we turned in our tent,
they started, the hundred flowing tightly,
one mind, up and over the west ridge,
gone, leaving us propped in the bowl,
the sky a blown phosphorescence,
no dream, no end, no question.

ACKNOWLEDGMENTS

"Manipulating the Innominates" and "Driving in Rain" appeared in *Poet Lore.*

"Stronger," "Rise vs.Run," "Acolytes," and "Urgency" appeared in *Field.*

"Two on a Shaman's Rattle" and "At Pacific Rim" appeared in *Willow Springs.*

"Anniversary" appeared in *Crab Creek Review.*

"Two Love Poems" appeared in *The Iowa Review.*

"Exploded View" appeared in *DoubleTake.*